# ELIGIBLE FOR AN UPGRADE

**DARLENE CAFFEY**

FOREWORD BY
BISHOP GARY HAWKINS, SR.

This book or parts thereof may not be reproduced in any form, stored in a retrieval system, or transmitted in any form by any means-electronic, mechanical, photocopy, recording or otherwise-without prior written permission of the publisher, except as provided by United States of America copyright law.

Copyright- © 2022 by: Darlene Caffey

All rights reserved

Cover artwork by: A.J. Hawkins
Photography by: David Ferebee
Printed by: Book Baby: Self Publishing, Book Printing & Distribution

Unless otherwise noted, all scriptures are taken from the King James Version

Print ISBN: 978-1-66782-959-3
eBook ISBN: 978-1-66782-960-9

# Foreword:
# Bishop Gary Hawkins, Sr. ~
# Voices of Faith Ministries

Ephesians 3: 20-21

*"And now unto Him who is able to do exceedingly, abundantly and above all that we ask or think, according to the power that works within us. $^{21}$ Unto Him be glory in the church by Christ Jesus throughout all ages, world without end." Amen.*

Technology is the one thing that is constant. It is always in change mode. When I was a teenager, we played music from an 8-track tape player and cassette tapes. When I grew into adulthood, we played music through CD's. Forty years later, we no longer use these technologies. They are now outdated. Today, technology is more fluid than ever. Many people today don't even download or buy music at all. Instead, they stream their favorite music from online services… Spotify, Pandora, Tidal, Apple Music, and more.

If the technology we use to enjoy our favorite music is fluid, constantly changing to give us a better experience, then, we too, as believers are in need of an upgrade. Our relationship with God does not start and end at the point of salvation. But as children of God, we are constantly growing in our faith to please God. In order to grow daily, we must be upgraded in every area of our lives. We must upgrade our faith in God. We must upgrade our prayer life. We must upgrade our commitment to serving God. Upgrading our relationships daily with God keeps us from being outdated in doing the will of God. Upgrades keep us in right standing with God. Upgrades keep us connected to God.

The greatest challenge for the believer is not his or her salvation, but it is constantly growing in Christ Jesus. We often become stagnated in our Christian walk with the Lord, because we stop growing in our knowledge of God. The moment you reach stagnation in Christ, you start to decrease activity in church. You make excuses for not attending Sunday morning worship. You justify your reason for no longer attending Bible Study. You blame others for your lack of participation in the many church auxiliaries. Your prayer life suffers. What has happened? You have distanced yourself from God. You are in need of an upgrade. You need to press the refresh button in your life to bring you back closer to Jesus Christ. This book, "Eligible For An Upgrade" by my spiritual daughter, Darlene Caffey, is a must read! She has just created a masterpiece. "Eligible For An Upgrade" is just what the doctor ordered. This book needed to be written, and it is well overdue for the body of Christ to embrace! Many believers are living stagnated lives daily, drifting farther away from God. This book is written for the believer and non-believer alike. Regardless of where you are spiritually *in your life, all of us are "Eligible For An Upgrade." All have sinned and fallen short of the glory of God. We sin daily by commission and omission, knowing and unknowing. "Eligible For An Upgrade" has the right antidote to refresh your life in the kingdom of God.*

*Sit back and buckle up, "Eligible For An Upgrade" is about to give you a strong signal with God. After reading this great book, your ears will be more attentive to the Holy Spirit than ever before. Your faith will reconnect with God to do great things in the kingdom of God. My prayer is that as you read this book, you rediscover a hunger, a zest, a zeal, and a passion for God like you have never experienced before. This book is the answer to many prayers. I declare that when you finish reading this amazing book, you will accept that you are "Eligible For An Upgrade"! Every man and woman should have this book in his or her library.*

*Bishop Gary Hawkins, Sr.*
*Founder and Senior Pastor*
*Voices of Faith Church, Stone Mountain, Ga.*

# Dedication Page

*This book is dedicated to the person who created, saved, and gave me the vision to write this book. He guided me from beginning to end, just as He has from my earliest existence to this present day. That person is none other than my Lord and Savior, Jesus Christ.*

*To my husband of 35 years, Ernest Caffey, Jr., for listening attentively to me as I speak and sing about Jesus throughout the day.*

*To my children, LaDeidra, Darius, Destiny, along with my daughter from another mother, Mehriya, and her oh so handsome and sweet son, Amir. I love you all so much!*

*To my siblings: Tanny, Aronita, Cynthia, Charles, Sandra and Caron who have supported me down through the years.*

*To Dr. Maury Wills and my DATE family who have believed in me since day 1.*

*To my friends both near and far who never stops encouraging me.*

*Last but not least, Bishop and Lady Gary Hawkins, Sr., and the Voices of Faith Family! What can I say? Thank you for believing in me! Bishop, it's the foreword for me, Sir!*

*Thank you all so much! Your love for me is so evident!*
*With Great Love,*
*Elder Darlene Caffey*

# CONTENTS

| | |
|---|---|
| Preface | 1 |
| "Read Your Text Messages" | 5 |
| "Unlimited Data" | 11 |
| "Caller ID" | 15 |
| "Invite Family and Friends" | 24 |
| "Free Wi-Fi" | 30 |
| "Not Just Any Server Will Do" | 32 |
| "Picture This" | 38 |
| "Utilize Your Delete Button" | 44 |
| "Face the Book" | 47 |
| "Keep Your Battery Charged" | 52 |
| "Watch What You Post" | 58 |
| "He's Never Outdated" | 62 |
| "He Keeps Track of Me | 65 |
| "Zoom Him In" | 69 |
| "GPS" (Guiding His People To Safety) | 72 |

# PREFACE

Like many of you, I'm a stickler for paying my bills on time. Well, on this particular day, I almost forgot that my cell phone bill was due. Not wanting to break my consistent streak, I quickly jumped out of bed, got dressed and headed to the store to satisfy my debt. Little did I know, this visit would change my life…forever!

As the attendant began pulling up my information, he presented me with startling news. "By the way," he exclaimed, "you do know you're eligible for an upgrade, right?" With a look of confusion upon my face, I suggested to him that there was no way in the world I was eligible, because I had allowed one of my children to talk me into using my upgrade for themselves. As we continued to exchange words, he said something else that would change my life… forever. He said, "If you don't believe me, I can show you." Turning the screen around for my view, with a look of confusion upon my face, I realized that he was right, and that I, indeed, was eligible for an upgrade.

Although I did not upgrade my phone that particular day, as I walked towards the door to leave, I received a message from the Holy Spirit Himself, indicating that not only was I eligible for an upgrade with my phone, (in the natural), but I was also eligible in the Spirit!!!! Come on somebody, and receive this word!! The devil has had you timid; he's had you second guessing yourself; he's told you that you would never get married again; he's told you that you would never experience marriage, he's told you that you were worthless; he's told you that you would never amount to anything; he's told you that you're wasting your time; he's told you that other people are better than you; he's told you to give up; he's told you to give in; he's told you to just throw in the towel; he's told you that because of your horrific, shameful past, you can never be forgiven; he's told you that because none of your family members graduated from college, that you wouldn't either; he's told you that you're wasting your time praying for your children because there's no hope for them! Well, can I suggest to you that the devil is a bald-faced liar, and the truth is not in him? Can I tell you that you're more anointed than you think you are? Can I tell you that you're smart, talented and beautiful? Can I tell you that you are needed in the body of Christ? Can I tell you that it doesn't matter where you started, but what matters is where you end? Can I tell you that there's a place for you in the kingdom? Can I tell you that you're not just a conqueror, but that you're "more than a conqueror?" (Romans 8:37). Can I tell you that the unpleasant place you find yourself in is not your final destination? Stop right there, and give Him praise!

God wants to move you from unsaved to saved, from ordinary to extraordinary, from less than to greater than, from defeat to victory, from pursuing fleshly desires to pursuing Godly desires, from making spending time in His Word not a duty but a delight, from relying on your own strength to relying on His strength, from tearing down to building up the body of Christ, from not your will, but His will be done, from what your friends think about a matter to what God KNOWS about a matter. God is saying that no matter your situation or circumstance, you are eligible for an upgrade. You meet the criteria to move from one level to the next level in Him and His Word. Are you ready to receive an upgrade? I had declined to get an upgrade on my phone, but I realized that an upgrade in my Spirit is far too valuable to decline. I have accepted my upgrade in the Spirit… How about you?

CHAPTER 1

# "READ YOUR TEXT MESSAGES"

*Psalm 119:105*

*"Thy Word is a lamp unto my feet, a light unto my path."*
*(Psalm 119:105).*

I'll never forget the day I learned to text! I felt like a kid at Christmas time. I also felt accomplished, because I never thought I'd master this feature. I'd watch my children text with such ease and quickness and decided that I'd rather do it the old-fashioned way and call. I learned though, that by using text messaging, I could receive responses within seconds or minutes. That was right up my alley, because many times I become impatient and can't wait. Well, there are times when God requires us to wait on Him, because only He knows the end from the beginning. Only He knows what's best for us; only He knows what lies ahead, and because of this, He teaches us lessons as we wait.

David had to wait on the Lord, and while he waited, he became a man after God's own heart. Open up your "text", and read the messages. He declared that, "The Lord is my shepherd, and I shall not want." (Psalm 23:1). He testified that, "Yea though I walk through the valley of the shadows of death, I will fear no evil." (Psalm 23:4). He could declare this with confidence because he had experience in waiting on the Lord, and he knew that the Lord would be with him. Open up your "text", and read the messages. When he knew that he had done wrong, he told the Lord to "Create in me a clean heart, O God; and renew a right spirit within me." (Psalm 51:10). He admitted to God that, "Against thee, thee alone have I sinned." (Psalm 51:4). He realized that the Lord was his "light and his salvation, so whom should he fear; that the Lord was the strength of his life, of whom should he be afraid, and also realized that, "in the time of trouble, God would hide him." (Psalm 27:1: 5). Has the Lord ever hidden you before? Has He ever shown you which way to go when your enemies were on your track? Has He ever been your shepherd? Has He ever exchanged your heart from madness to gladness? I mean, have you ever just checked out the text and realized that His love for you is not contingent upon your love for Him?

Have you ever just been in a place where you just wanted to delight yourself in Him? Have you ever been in a place where you just had to encourage yourself in the Lord because the people you thought would support you didn't because they felt that you were in way over your head? Read your text, and Paul will let you know in

Philippians 4:13 that, "You can do ALL things through Christ who strengthens you." Open up your text and read Romans 8:18 where Paul reminds us that, "I reckon that the sufferings of this present time are not worthy to be compared to the glory which shall be revealed in us."

When you open up your Word, you will find that there's peace on the other side of your storm, joy in the midst of your sorrow, deliverance in the midst of your depression, a testimony for your test, and a message for your mess. The devil absolutely hates it when you open up your text because you will begin to discover who you really are and whose you really are. He doesn't want you to discover that, "For our light affliction, which is but for a moment, worketh for us a far more exceeding and eternal weight of glory." (2 Corinthians 4:17). He's afraid that your eyes will be opened and that you'll begin to see things in the Spirit. He's shaking because he knows that your ears will be opened and inclined unto the Lord. He's nervous that if you seek God and open up your mouth and give Him praise, the Holy Spirit will reveal that, "He that believeth on me, as the scripture hath said, out of your belly shall flow rivers of living waters." (John 7:38). He's afraid that you will experience joy unspeakable and full of glory." (Peter 1:8). He's afraid that the Lord will wipe away your salty tears and turn your tears of defeat into tears of victory. Yes, Lord!

My dad was a Southern Baptist Minister who spent much time in God's Word. I can remember him sitting down with me teaching me scriptures. The very first passage he taught me was Psalm 100.

When I learned it, he would call on me to present it in front of church, or at prayer meetings. Back then, I could memorize things really well; now, the Holy Spirit takes on a whole new meaning. Before I knew it, I started truly making a joyful noise unto the Lord. Before I knew it, I started serving Him with gladness because I had to experience my upgrade, you see. I had to go from depending on my dad reading the scriptures with me, to becoming independent enough to read on my own.

Well, Daddy's gone now, but he instilled God's Word in me so that I could live the life God has planned for me. He knew that when He was long gone, God's Word would sustain, protect and rebuke me when needed, so I quickly found out that I needed His Word everyday. I learned how to live and forgive by reading His Word. I also found out that, through His Word, I would see Daddy again someday, but until then, I must take full responsibility for the fact that it isn't about me, but it's about God. I learned in I Peter 9:10 that I was a "chosen vessel and a royal priesthood." I learned that my Father owned everything, even "a cattle on a thousand hills." (Psalm 50: 5b). I learned that, "But my God would supply all of my needs according to His riches in glory in Christ Jesus. (Philippians 4:19). I learned that if I was lonely, that He would be my comforter and friend that sticks closer than any brother. I learned that, "For in the time of trouble, He shall hide me in His pavilion." (Psalm 27:5). I learned that He would be my mother after my mother was gone; He would be my sister, after my sister was gone; He would be my brother after my brother was gone. I learned that I could depend on Him when man misunderstood me. I learned that I could rest in Him when my body seems to wear out. I learned that if I would just be still, and let Him fight my battles, He would do just that for me. I learned to "Fret not myself because of evildoers, because they would soon be cut off." (Psalm 37:1), to, "Delight myself in Him, and He would give me the desires of my heart," (Psalm 37:5), that, "Even from everlasting to everlasting, thou art God",( Psalm 90: 2b) that, "There's none like unto thee." (Jeremiah 10:6). I also discovered how to allow God to, "Stir up the gift that is within me." (2 Timothy 1:6). Can you stop for about ten seconds and give Him praise?

Many times, we skip over text messages and read them later, but what if God has a message for you right now, but you're too tired to open up your text and read it? What if you can be healed, delivered and set free from torment just by opening up your Word? What if He has a message of hope and love just for you for such a time as this? What if He's trying to tell you right now how to receive your upgrade? What if you opened your text and found out that tithing isn't so bad after all? What if you found out that if you "Give, He'll give it back to you, and it will be a good measure, pressed down, shaken together and running over?" (Luke 6:38). What if you accepted that forgiveness is a requirement and not an option? What if you learned through His Word that you have power over the serpent, and that you could speak to your mountain and it would have to "move and be cast into the sea?" (Mark 11:23.) What if you just took a chance and opened up your text and realized that, "The weapons of your warfare are not carnal but mighty through the pulling down of strongholds?" (2 Corinthians 10:4). I can assure you that if you just open up your text, you will be astonished at what you will find. If you open up your text, you will discover peace like a river which flows continually; you will experience hope for a better tomorrow; you'll find that He will wipe away your tears, and you'll rest better at night; not only that, but you'll want to treat others right! Open up your text, and see how powerful you are. Open up your text so that secrets can be revealed and generational curses can be broken, and find how your family members can be saved and stay saved. Open up your text, and see what He has in store for you. Open up your text, and "Taste and see that the Lord is good, and that His mercies endure forever more." (Psalm 34:8a).

CHAPTER 2

# "UNLIMITED DATA"

*Jeremiah 33:3*

*'Call on Me, and I will answer you, and I will tell you great and mighty things, which you do not know."*

My youngest daughter, Destiny, is on the same cell phone plan as her dad's. I often hear him tell her not to use up all of his data because once she goes over the limit, it becomes costly. Has she ever gone over her limit before? She certainly has. Does her dad scold her? You bet he does. Imagine having to get in touch with Jesus at certain times. Imagine Him telling us that our data usage is about to run out and that we'd have to wait for the next month for it to start over again. Imagine Him telling us that the weekends will cost more to get in touch with Him. Imagine the life-line to Him failing after you've used up your Spiritual Data.

I'm so glad that He has time for me whenever I call Him. I'm so glad that there's no limit as to when I can call Him. I'm so glad that when I can't sleep at night from the cares of this world that I can call on Him, and not only will He hear me, He will also answer. I'm so glad that He dries my tears in the midnight hour when my body is racked with pain; yet, He never makes me feel that He's too busy to attend to my needs. I'm so glad that He's a waymaker who never fails. I'm so glad that, "The blessings of the Lord maketh rich, and He addeth no sorrow with it." (Proverbs 10:22). He's so good that He will even wake us up late at night and call us by our name. If you don't believe me, ask Samuel, who was living with Eli in the temple after his mother Hannah promised God that if he would give her a son, she would give him back and that "no razor would come upon his head." (1 Samuel 1:11). Samuel thought that it was Eli calling him because the Word of the Lord had not yet been revealed to him, so Samuel ran to Eli a first time, a second time, and finally, a third time, thinking it was Eli who called him. Eli told Samuel that when the Lord called on him that third time, to answer in these words: "Speak, for thy servant heareth." (1 Samuel 3:10).

Not only do I have unlimited calls, but I can also access the internet or youtube to hear a song from Vikki Winans who will remind me that, "We Shall Behold Him." I can download Yolanda Adams encouraging me to , "Never Give Up!" I can log on and hear Erica Campbell tell me that she's "Praying For Me." I can switch over and hear a Word from my Bishop, Gary Hawkins, Sr., declaring that,

"I Got Next," or from my former Bishop and friend, the Honorable Bishop Gregory Wells describe, "A Gourmet's Delight," or T.D. Jakes reminding me that, "He Still Wants Me." Since there's no limit on when, where or how long I can use my data, I am determined to use it up! I will use it to have prayer with my family during the weekday at 6:00 A.M., I'll use it on the fourth Saturdays to go to the pit with my family to intercede for others.

I don't have to wait for the church doors to open back up to give Him praise. I don't have to wait for my favorite song to be played in order to lift up my hands and give Him praise. I don't have to wait for the pastor to make his way to the pulpit to worship Him in Spirit and in truth because I have "unlimited data!" When I'm sick and can't get in touch with anyone, I can lay my hands on myself and speak the Word of faith over my own life. When I'm weak, I can call on Jesus, the rock in a weary land. When I've messed up, I can contact Him anytime and ask that He forgives and cleanses me. Do you have unlimited data? If not, simply confess with your mouth, and believe in your heart that God raised Jesus from the dead, and you SHALL be saved, (Romans 10: 9), anytime, any place, or anywhere!

Well, there are some people who never use this feature called, "unlimited data." Perhaps, this is because they don't know that it's available. Perhaps, they feel like they have to have a certain status in the kingdom. Perhaps, they feel like their sins are too great. Perhaps, someone else has kicked them out of the place that God anointed them to be, and they were made to believe that they were beneath others. Honey, let me tell you something. We've all sinned and fallen short of the glory of God! God knew we were going to mess up; that's why He wouldn't come down from the cross. He could have come down at any time, but He had me on His mind; He had you on His mind. He had our filthiest sins on His mind. He had to fulfill His Father's will. He had to take the stripes and endure the pain. He had to die so that He could live again. Hallelujah to Jesus! Even when He desired for the cup to pass, He still said, "Nevertheless, not my will, but thine be done." (Luke 22:42 b). Come on here somebody!! What if He had come down? Where would we be? Who would we turn to when the storms of life are raging? Who would we tell all about our troubles? Who would rock us to sleep at night when we're overwhelmed with debt problems and family problems and work problems and marital problems and children problems and just problems? Who would raise up a standard against our enemies when they attack us mercilessly? Use your data, my sister! Use your data, my brother! I don't care what time of day it is. I don't care if it's a holiday, use your data. It's unlimited, and you have the right to use it anytime you want. Use it during good times. Use it during troubled times. He died for this. He longs for this. Don't disappoint Him by not using this much needed feature; your life will change forever!

## CHAPTER 3

# "CALLER ID"

*1 Thessalonians 5:24*

*"Faithful is He that calleth you, who also will do it."*

Can you admit that there are times when someone calls you late in the midnight hour or early in the morning time, but you just don't feel like receiving their call? How many times has someone called you and it was the wrong number? If you're like me, I rarely answer my phone when I don't recognize the number. On one occasion, I did receive an unknown caller's call, but this time, I felt compelled to answer. On the other end was a woman who was in distress. She was broken. She needed a word. She needed to be encouraged, and I knew immediately that the Holy Spirit had orchestrated this chance encounter.

As we began to speak, the Lord began to take over the conversation. She began to share that her marriage was in complete despair. She was trying to make sense of her life, but didn't know where to turn. She needed to talk, cry and be set free. After our initial conversation, we developed a mother/daughter relationship, and we began to pray together each morning. Her children and I developed a relationship as well, and I was able to see the Lord open doors for them as well.

I often wonder what would have happened if I had not obeyed the Holy Spirit and answered this call. Would the young lady have just given up? Would the next person she called be available? Would they have given her Spiritual advice? Would they have taken the time to pray with her? More importantly, would they have kept in touch with her, or would they have ignored her call each time they saw her number pop up on their caller ID? This is exactly what can happen when we don't allow the Holy Spirit to lead and guide us. We may be the very person that God wants to use to pull someone else through difficult times. God may even use you as a resource for others to point them into the right direction. Even if you don't know the direction to point an individual in, you may know someone else who does.

I love the story of Saul on the Road to Damascus. (Acts 9). And Saul, yet breathing out threatenings and slaughter against the disciples of the Lord, went unto the high priest, [2] And desired of him letters to Damascus to the synagogues, that if he found any of this way, whether they were men or women, he might bring them bound unto Jerusalem. [3] And as he journeyed, he came near Damascus:

and suddenly, there shined round about him a light from heaven: ⁴ And he fell to the earth, and heard a voice saying unto him, "Saul, Saul, why persecutest thou me?"

⁵ And he said, "Who art thou, Lord?" And the Lord said, "I am Jesus whom thou persecutest: it is hard for thee to kick against the pricks." ⁶ And he trembling and astonished said, "Lord, what wilt thou have me to do?" And the Lord said unto him, "Arise, and go into the city, and it shall be told thee what thou must do." ⁷ And the men who journeyed with him stood speechless, hearing a voice, but seeing no man. ⁸ And Saul arose from the earth; and when his eyes were opened, he saw no man: but they led him by the hand, and brought him into Damascus. ⁹ And he was without sight for three days, and neither did eat nor drink.¹⁰ And there was a certain disciple at Damascus, named Ananias; and to him said the Lord in a vision, "Ananias." And he said, "Behold, I am here, Lord." ¹¹ So the Lord *said* to him, "Arise and go to the street called Straight, and inquire at the house of Judas for *one* called Saul of Tarsus, for behold, he is praying. ¹² And in a vision, he has seen a man named Ananias coming in and putting *his* hand on him, so that he might receive his sight."

¹³ Then Ananias answered, "Lord, I have heard from many about this man, how much harm he has done to Your saints in Jerusalem. ¹⁴ And here he has authority from the chief priests to bind all who call on Your name." ¹⁵ But the Lord said to him, "Go, for he is a chosen vessel of Mine to bear My name before Gentiles, kings,

and the children of Israel. ¹⁶ For I will show him how many things he must suffer for My name's sake."¹⁷ And Ananias went his way and entered the house; and laying his hands on him he said, "Brother Saul, the Lord Jesus, who appeared to you on the road as you came, has sent me that you may receive your sight and be filled with the Holy Spirit." ¹⁸ Immediately there fell from his eyes *something* like scales, and he received his sight at once; and he arose and was baptized. ¹⁹ So when he had received food, he was strengthened. Then Saul spent some days with the disciples at Damascus.

There are several things which intrigued me about this passage. Here, you have Saul, who wanted nothing to do with God. He had heard of His signs and wonders, but still had no desire to get to know Him. What I love even more though, is the fact that God didn't treat Saul the same way. That'll preach right there! Instead, God, after knowing what Saul had done to others; after knowing that he was on his way to get permission to persecute anyone he saw on his way that believed in the living God, God never retaliated. What if God had considered Saul a lost cause? What if He had given Saul what He deserved? Although Saul considered God an "unknown caller," God decided to save Him anyway. Not only did He knock him off his horse and blind him for 3 days, He already had someone in place who not only nourished him back to health, but baptized him as well. What you say???? Not only did he receive his sight back in the physical, but his Spiritual eyes were also opened. He goes from wanting to insult the disciples to wanting to sup with them. Won't

God do it? He went from not wanting to read the Word to writing 28% of the New Testament. He went from being a snake to shaking off snakes. He went from Saul to Paul because God didn't just change his mind, He changed his name. He went from not having a desire to witness, to witnessing so much until you couldn't shut him up. He went from not respecting the anointing to becoming anointed, so much so that according to Acts 19:12, "So that from his body were brought unto the sick handkerchiefs or aprons, and the diseases departed from them, and the evil spirits departed from them."

Even when he was in prison with Silas for preaching and teaching the Gospel, instead of having a "woe it's me spirit," they sang and prayed to God, and the very foundation of the jail began to shake until the doors were open, and they were all set free. Help me praise Him somebody!!!! He went from not caring that he was a sinner to admitting to being the chiefest of sinners. He went from taking pleasure in harming others to taking pleasure in his own infirmities, reproaches, necessities, persecutions and distresses for Christ's sake: "For when I am weak," he declared, "then am I strong." ( 2 Corinthians 12:10). He went from relying on His own strength to relying on God's strength when He declared in Philippians 4:13 that, "I can do all things through Christ which gives me strength." He went from not moving forward with the devil to "pressing toward the mark for the High Call in Christ Jesus." (Philippians 3:14). Glory to God! Can somebody praise Him with me right there? Who can do that but God?

The way He leads us may not always be popular or convenient for us, but trust me when I say that God knows what to do, when to do it, and how to do it. We must trust Him at ALL times, and we must NEVER, EVER leave Him out of our decisions, take advantage of His goodness, or get to a place where we feel as if we have arrived and no longer need Him. In short, we should never travel this road of life without asking Him to lead us because He knows just how to lead us to the path of righteousness, and since He also knows just how much we can bear, He alone knows just how to restore us. The word restoration itself simply means to renew. Oftentimes, the devil leads us to believe that we can't be restored, but God wants us to come back to Him. Well Elder, I'm an adulterer; well, repent, and find your way back to Him. Well Elder, I'm a fornicator. Repent, and allow Him to deliver you. Well Elder, I have a lying tongue. Repent, and allow Him to give you a tongue of praise. Well Elder, I'm a murderer. Repent, and receive His forgiveness. Well, I'm a drug dealer; in fact, I smoke more than I deal. Repent, and He will receive you with open arms, and as the prodigal son did to his son, He won't even mention what you've done, where you've been, who you've been with, or how long you were gone. Heaven will rejoice in the fact that you realized you are safer with Jesus; you realized that there had to be a better life for you; you had to realize that if you remained in the shape that you were in, your sins would soon overtake you.

When we can't make sense of what's going on around us, He already knows, and He has the solution to every one of our problems. When Paul testifies about the previously mentioned scripture in 2 Corinthians 12:10 that, "Therefore I take pleasure in infirmities, in reproaches, in necessities, in persecutions, in distresses for Christ's sake: for when I am weak, then am I strong," it should be noted that the reason Paul was able to make such a bold statement was because he knew from where his strength derived. He knew that he could not depend on his own strength because it would give out. This is the reason he also admits in Romans 7: 8 that, "For I know that in me (that is, in my flesh,) dwelleth no good thing: for to will is present with me; but how to perform that which is good I find not. [19] For the good that I would I do not: but the evil which I would not, that I do. [20] Now if I do that I would not, it is no more I that do it, but sin that dwelleth in me. [21] I find then a law, that, when I would do good, evil is present with me."

Paul didn't have to be in a particular location to communicate with God. Naw! He was on the road to Damascus when he had an encounter with God. His flesh despised God, that's why he was on his way to Damascus to kill anyone who served the Lord. It took him to experience a "turning point" before he denied his flesh and took up his cross to follow Jesus. He wasn't in a physical church building when he escaped to the island called Melita and ended up with a group of barbarians who thought little of him and showed little kindness. Acts 28:3 suggests that, "Because of the contrary weather, they created a fire, and as Paul gathered a bundle of sticks and laid *them* on the fire, there came a viper out of the heat, and fastened on his hand. ⁴And when the barbarians saw the *venomous* beast hang on his hand, they said among themselves, "No doubt this man is a murderer, whom, though he hath escaped the sea, yet vengeance suffereth him not to live.⁵ And he shook off the beast into the fire, and felt no harm."

⁶"Howbeit they looked when he should have swollen, or fallen down dead suddenly: but after they had looked a great while, and saw no harm come to him, they changed their minds, and said that he was a "god." Take the three Hebrew boys, for example. These fellas were placed in a fiery furnace; yet, they did not depend on their flesh to deliver them out; they instead depended on the Lord, and He delivered them. They didn't back down either, but they spoke boldly to the king, declaring to him that even if God didn't deliver them to not get it twisted, because He was still "able".

I remember years ago when my husband was in the military. I accepted a job outside of my comfort zone, and was eventually let go. I remember telling my then boss that God had something better for me. Three weeks later, I received a job outside of the base teaching English to Japanese citizens. I would ride the train 3 hours a day to get to my destination. That didn't matter to me because I knew that I was in the right place at the right time. The money was about triple what I was making before. My stress level was down. I smiled more and met some of the nicest people I had ever met.

It was all because of my "wifi" connection. I spoke the Word, and God honored me. He moved me out of what wasn't meant for me into what was meant for me. He gave me an increase when I spoke the Word. He gave me a peace of mind when I spoke the Word. He was on the train with me for those 3 hours going back and forth on the train and placed me in the midst of people who knew and appreciated my worth.

That's why I can't afford to get all bent out of shape when one job doesn't work out. I count it as joy because I know that obviously, God has something better for me. I rejoice, and again I tell you I rejoice because I know that there's nothing like being in the place where God anointed and appointed you to be. They can pass out all the pink slips they want, but when I'm walking in the path that God has chosen for me, even if I am the last hired, God will turn the tide in my favor. I don't care if there's a freeze on hiring. I believe God will unfreeze the hiring process just for me. I don't care if it's never been done before, oh well, I guess there's a first time for everything. I don't care if I'm not qualified for the position, if God sent me, He will qualify me. He will justify me. He will teach me. He will prosper me. He'll have the boss saying, "I don't understand why I'm doing this, but something on the inside is telling me to not let you go. In fact, whatever it is, or whomever it is, they're also telling me to give you a raise." Man, I wish I had a witness!

## CHAPTER 4

# "INVITE FAMILY AND FRIENDS"

*Matthew 11:28*

*"Come unto me, all ye who labour and are heavy laden, and I will give you rest."*

Another unique feature of a cell phone is that you can invite family and friends to join your line. Ok! I felt something right there. Whenever I talk to my family and friends, somewhere in the conversation, the name of the Lord is sure to come up. I breathe Him. I wake up with Him on my mind. I go to bed each night thinking about Him. I literally think about Him all day long!!!!! Well, if He means that much to me, and I want others to experience His love, why would I keep this incredible news to myself? I simply refuse to do that because I love to brag about Jesus. I've written over 100 poems bragging about Him. I share my testimonies with anyone who will listen because I need to let them know that if God did it for me, He can certainly do it for them. I share how God came to me in a vision one night, and I invite them into that vision to remind them that God has not forgotten about us. I share how when I was a little girl who wandered from her backyard only to encounter a snake coming toward me from across the street, but God sent an angel in the form of a man in a truck to run over the snake just in time. I share how my daddy would take me to pray at prayer band meetings on Thursday nights whether I wanted to go or not. I share how I almost died in my dorm room, but God kept me alive for such a time as this. I share how God sent an old woman to rescue me when a Doberman Pinscher tried to chase after me from the other side of the road. I share that when I had the desire and not the confidence to become a teacher; yet, God led me to the right place at the right time, and some 27 years later, He still anoints me to reach and teach students. I share how the Lord kept me even when my husband and I lived in Japan. I share that "He's a very present help in times of trouble." (Psalm 46b).

I invite others in by showing my vulnerability. I invite others in by letting them know that despite the rumors that Christianity is boring and that God no longer performs miracles, it's just what it's called…a rumor. Unfortunately, many prefer hearing a rumor rather than the truth because it prevents us from being committed and accountable. There were many rumors about Jesus which stemmed from His death to His resurrection. It was doubted that He could be born without physical conception. It was doubted that He was the son of God. Thomas doubted Him although he had witnessed His miracles for three long years. (John 20:24–29). "But Thomas, one of the twelve, called Didymus, was not with them when Jesus came. [27] Then saith He to Thomas, "Reach hither thy finger, and behold My hands; and reach hither thy hand, and thrust it into My side: and be not faithless, but believing." Jesus invited him to touch Him in order that he might believe.

There are just some people who have to be shown before they believe, but what happened to walking by faith and not by sight? Why is it easier for us to believe someone who calls us with a scam promising us wealth if we would give out our personal information instead of taking God at His word? Why can't we just take what He says to heart and receive it by faith? You do know that according to Hebrews 11:6 that, "Without faith, it's impossible to please Him, right? You do know that, "Now faith is the substance of things hoped for and the evidence of things not seen, right? (Hebrews 11:16), and you do believe that only faith moves God, right?

Now granted, there are some family and friends who may not want to join your Spiritual line because they may feel it's too costly. They may feel like they'll be missing out on something or they may have to give up worldly pleasures. The common denominator in this equation is "flesh"! At what point are we going to take ourselves out of the equation and realize that it is He who gives us the will and the do of His good pleasure; (Philippians 2:13). Jeremiah 29:11 encourages us by telling us, "For I know the thoughts that I think toward you, saith the Lord, thoughts of peace, and not of evil, to give you an expected end." That's good news!

Well, how do you invite family and friends? The simplest way is to live a life before them that they will want to accept your invitation. Matthew 7:16 suggests that, "Ye shall know them by their fruit." [22] Not only that, but Galatians 5:22-23 emphasizes that, "But the fruit of the Spirit is love, joy, peace, longsuffering, gentleness, goodness, faith, [23] Meekness, temperance: against such there is no law." Well, how do we demonstrate this fruit amongst family and friends when we're having issues as well? We hold fast to our beliefs and refuse to compromise. Speak when He tells you to speak. Listen when He tells you to listen. Consider yourself and your own faults first. Allow them to see your blessings. Allow them to feel your heart, and emphasize that they can come to you with their problems knowing that you are going to pray for them and believe with them that God will change their circumstances.

I can't tell you the number of times I've witnessed to back-slidden friends or loved ones, or those family or friends who have never made a full commitment to Christ, wait to see how I respond to certain situations. I can't tell you how they catch themselves and say things like, "Oh, I forgot you were a Christian." A funny situation happened to me recently that made me realize that even my students know my stance with Christ. I gave an assignment worth several points this past school year. The students worked really hard to do well on these assignments. I advised them to meet me on Zoom at a certain time with questions. Two students met me because they wanted to know if they could include something "religious" in their project. I immediately knew which student came up with this bright idea. When I called the student out, all he could do was shake his head. I even told him exactly what he had said, which was, "Mrs. Caffey is a Christian, so if we add something about Jesus in our project, we'll probably get extra points." Talk about kmsl! (killing myself laughing)! So, you just never know who's watching you; therefore, you should never look like what you're going through when you're inviting friends and family to follow you as you follow Christ. Don't allow them to see you act unseemly even when times are hard. If they talk about you, it's ok, just don't compromise. If they don't invite you over, that's okay, too. If they snicker when you come around, let them snicker. If they call you "holy roller," that's cool, too, but at least they know whose side you're on. Sooner or later, the very ones who tested your faith will be the same ones who will call you when life hits them, but remember not to bring that up. Simply pray for them, and after you have prayed, invite them to become a part of the body of Christ. Read scriptures with and to them. Remind them that they're not a misfit, that though they made mistakes along the way, God can still use them for His glory. Remind them that life is worth living and that they can prosper even as their souls prosper. Never cease to be available to them when they are in need.

Granted, sometimes family and friends are skeptical about sharing information to those close to them because they fear it getting out to other family and friends. I pride myself in keeping information shared with me to myself. I believe that if that person wanted you to know, they would have contacted you. What am I saying? Let's practice trustworthiness because the last thing you want to do is to invite a friend to get to know the Jesus you claim to know, yet they deny your invitation because you've invited too many others to be a part of their personal issues.

It took me a while to learn that news travels fast, especially if it's unfortunate news. I want to be that person that when you share something with me that I don't share with others. I never want to be in a position where someone approaches me because I shared their personal information. I never want to be the reason that someone else loses confidence in others. I never want to be in a position where I'm confronted for not being able to hold water. I want others to be able to come to me and rest assuredly that their business won't end up on the local news.

## CHAPTER 5

# "FREE WI-FI"

*Psalm 139:7-10*
*King James Version*

*[7] Whither shall I go from thy spirit? or whither shall I flee from thy presence. [8] If I ascend up into heaven, thou art there: if I make my bed in hell, behold, thou art there. [9] If I take the wings of the morning, and dwell in the uttermost parts of the sea; [10] Even there shall thy hand lead me, and thy right hand shall hold me.*

I believe that Wi-Fi is one of the most beneficial features of all! Not only is it good for students who may be doing homework, but it's also good when you are traveling, for making calls and much more.

In some instances, you are limited as to where you can utilize your wi-fi. Thank God this is not the case with Him. I don't have to worry about whether a hotel is going to allow me free Wi-Fi when I go on vacation with my family or friends. I don't have to worry about if I have to be in a "hot spot" to reach Heaven. No!! The Holy Ghost is a "hot spot" all within Himself, and since He lives in me and moves in me, and He's everywhere I go, my Spiritual "wi-fi" will never be compromised.

Isn't it funny how technology has come along and changed the entire course of our very existence? It's everywhere, and it doesn't discriminate where age, gender or geographics are concerned. Losing your Wi-Fi can actually cause uncontrollable frustration if we're not careful. When we consider this scenario in the Spirit, several scriptures should come to mind. Take Psalms 46:1, for example. David knew God to be our "refuge and strength, an ever-present help in trouble." Isaiah 41:10 also encourages us when He states, "So do not fear, for I am with you; do not be dismayed, for I am your God. I will strengthen you and help you; I will uphold you with my righteous right hand." Just because Wi-fi may not always be available to us naturally, when we take God at His word, spend time in His presence and acknowledge Him in all of our ways, we can reach Him wherever we are.

# CHAPTER 6

# "NOT JUST ANY SERVER WILL DO"

*Psalm 100: 2-4*
*King James Version*

*[2] Serve the Lord with gladness: come before His presence with singing. [3] Know ye that the Lord He is God: it is He that hath made us, and not we ourselves; we are His people, and the sheep of His pasture. [4] Enter into His gates with thanksgiving, and into His courts with praise: be thankful unto Him, and bless His name.*

There is an ongoing debate about which cell phone server is best. Some prefer Sprint, while others prefer Verizon. Some are satisfied with T-Mobile, and some are content with AT&T. We select servers based on several factors: price, data usage, picture clarity and more. Oftentimes in church, we compare one ministry over the next. We prefer one singer over the next. We prefer one preacher over another. The word server, however, simply means to serve. The server, (the noun), is the one who serves, (the verb). What God is calling for is someone to serve Him in Spirit and in truth. In order to serve Him in Spirit and in truth, we have to walk by the "Spirit so that we do not fulfill the lust of our flesh." (Galatians 5:16). When we serve in Spirit, we are able to discern the needs of others, speak what God tells us to speak, and listen when He tells us to listen. We are able to love those who never knew love by our tender concern for them. Thus, we are able to lead others to Christ in a manner that makes them excited to know the Lord we serve. How cool is that?

Serving is not just limited to church. We serve in our homes, on jobs such as restaurant workers, teachers, personal trainers, and more. The way we serve is crucially important because it is the manner in which we serve which will determine whether or not others will want us to serve them again. It can determine whether or not someone will leave you a tip or give you a positive review. It can determine whether or not others will come to you for Spiritual advice. Well, how can I serve others when I need to be served myself? You might ask. I can tell you that there have been times in my life when I've felt the same way. I didn't feel like serving, but I knew that someone else's breakthrough or success was contingent upon my ability to serve in Spirit and truth. I may have wanted to cry at times because of my personal dilemmas, but I had to find a way to smile if just for a while. I have to always remind myself that no matter what I'm going through, someone else is worse off and would love to trade places with me; that although I may have wept during the night, my morning joy was sure to come. That's why I make it a point to keep a smile on my face despite what I'm going through. That's why others know me by my happy persona, because I strive to not look like what I'm going through. It may only take a "Good Morning, how are you today?" It may even take a word of inspiration... that's serving. It may take you to just listen to someone else. This is also considered serving.

My 10th grader recently received a job where she will have to serve others. In my motherly advice, I challenged her to smile at her customers, to speak kindly to them and to let them know that she was happy to be their server. I advised her to never allow her personal issues to interfere with serving others. My reason for sharing this with her is because if she does these things, customers will want to come back. Not only will they come back, but they will bring someone else along with them. I took it a step further and told her how they will become inspired by her and even give her a good review. They'll ask the boss where you are if you happen to be off that day, and in my daughter's case, they'll gladly leave you a tip.

I often encounter those who admit to me that they could never be a teacher because they don't have the patience for kids. "Well," I think to myself, "You probably couldn't, because teaching is about servitude." My sole purpose for teaching has and always will be, "to touch a life forever." I'm always willing to inspire students to the point that they recognize their talents, abilities and strengths. I allow each student to present projects of their choice to celebrate a unit so that they can feel good about themselves. By doing this, I've been able to witness students who hated school ending up loving it, and students who hated writing becoming my best writers. You see, a true servant has to consider others before themselves. Not only that, but a true servant also realizes that they don't have to always be in the spotlight in order to shine. A true servant will show others how to serve. A true servant will be willing to go that extra mile to make others feel special, needed and wanted. A true servant serves God with all of their heart, mind, soul and Spirit. A true servant considers other people's feelings. A true servant doesn't take his/her problems out on others. A true servant doesn't even bring his problems to the workplace. A true servant speaks to others, even if they don't speak back. A true servant yearns for the opportunity to serve. He spots out those who need encouragement, and he does it without motives. A true servant will follow up with you to see if you're ok. A true servant will take your call in the middle of the night. A true servant will call on the name of Jesus on your behalf. Jesus Himself came to serve. Mark 10:45 shares that, "For even the Son of Man came not to be served but to serve, and to give His life as a ransom for many." If the almighty God, whom we should be serving, came to serve, what does that say to us? To me, it suggests that anyone can serve at any time, but we must do it willingly.

My dad wouldn't have it any other way. He demonstrated and demanded faithful servitude from all 9 of his children by making us spend the night with the elderly and taking them to the store, or in my grandmother's case, to the check exchange when her monthly check arrived. She referred to it as, "the round coming around." We didn't have a choice in whether or not we'd serve her. It was one of the greatest forms of servitude I've ever experienced. Even today, I look to serve the elderly. I love hearing their stories. I love having them teach me. I love it when they give me sound advice. I love it when they give me pointers on cooking and marriage and raising my children.

I'll never forget the day I met the late, great Mother Bessie Powell at Voices of Faith Ministries some years ago. I had been waiting for God to send me an elderly person to serve- someone who would help groom me by sharing their wisdom. I noticed her at church one Sunday morning and thought, "She looks exactly like my Head Start School teacher, Mrs. Elnora. Running over to her with arms stretched wide, I asked, "Will you be my mom?" She later told me that she was wondering who this big eyed woman was jumping over folk to get to her. Mother Powell and I were simply inseparable. In fact, I told my friends shortly after meeting her to not call me on Saturdays from 8:00 A.M. to at least 12 noon because that was the time Mother Powell and I would be doing our running around. She was so sharp during the time I knew her, and could she cook? I shall never forget the time she invited me to dinner for the first time. You would have thought she was cooking for an army. There was so much food, from spaghetti to chicken to ribs to greens, and she even made dessert. What I loved most about the food was that I knew immediately that it had been cooked with the most important ingredient of all…Love!! This is the kind of service God is pleased with. I mean, anybody can serve, but do you truly serve others just because it's a job to you, or do you serve to make a lasting impact on others? We get weak physically, mentatlly and emotionally at times; yet, He knows and cares. We get upset at times when things don't happen when we think they should happen. We become discouraged and want to give up because it seems like others around us have it going on, and we find ourselves questioning God over and over again, wondering when our change will come. One thing I know about God is that He's an on-time God. There have been times when I expected Him to come at a particular time, but He came in His own time; yet, it was right on time. Sometimes, He used someone else to pour into my life. He sent someone else to encourage me. He sent someone else to bless me. He sent someone else to tell me to hold on just a little while longer. It just so happens that every person He sent my way was willing to serve me in any capacity I needed. Not only that, but they left a lasting impression on me to the point where I want to do the same.

## CHAPTER 7

# "PICTURE THIS"

*John 11*
*King James Version 11*

*Now a certain man was sick, named Lazarus, of Bethany, the town of Mary and her sister Martha. ² (It was that Mary who anointed the Lord with ointment, and wiped his feet with her hair, whose brother Lazarus was sick.) ³ Therefore his sisters sent unto him, saying, Lord, behold, he whom thou lovest is sick. ⁴ When Jesus heard that, he said, This sickness is not unto death, but for the glory of God, that the Son of God might be glorified thereby.*

Picture this! Lazarus, the brother of Mary and Martha, dead for four days. Picture this… Jesus calling him forth to live again. This would be the last miracle Jesus would perform before the Passover. Mary and Martha called on Jesus because they knew that if there was any chance of Lazarus living again, it would take a miracle from his friend, the healer, Jesus. Picture yourself in a dead situation where there seems to be no hope of life. Picture Jesus loving you so much, as He did Lazarus, telling you to rise up. Picture Him telling those around to "loosen" you. Picture yourself coming out of your situation right now, not looking like your situation, with your enemies thinking that you're dead because you seem to have no form of life, and life as you know it exists no more. One thing that moved me about this story is the fact that Jesus already knew that Lazarus would rise again, but the lack of faith from others could have also made Him doubt. That's why you have to be very careful who you talk to by faith, because not everyone walks by faith. Martha even mentioned that if Jesus had been there, her brother would not have died; yet, Jesus didn't have to be there. In fact, the scripture declares that he stayed where he was for 2 days before he began traveling back to Bethany. Martha, still puzzled, misunderstood what Jesus meant when she thought Jesus was referring to the resurrection when He assured her that Lazarus would rise again. He had to remind her that He was the resurrection and the life. Oh yes, He is the one who was and is and is to come. That's why we can't put Him in a little bottle. That's why we can't limit Him because He can do what He wants to do whenever He wants to do it. What I love about Him is that He will restore you right in the midst of naysayers. He'll even have doctors shaking their heads at His miracles. He'll have your enemies counting you out, when Jesus is counting you in.

Yes, you may have on your grave clothes, and yes, you may have a napkin covering your mouth, but like Lazarus, Jesus is calling you by your name telling you to come forth! Come forth in your ministry! Come forth in your healing! Come forth in your finances! Come forth in your mind! Come forth in your Spirit! Come forth in your deliverance! Come forth and cause your enemies to ask, "What must I do to be saved?"

Now, picture Calvary. The place where Jesus would willingly take on the sins of the entire world. He was an innocent man who only wanted to do His Father's will. The only way He could do this was to take the worst beating known to man and the worst torture anyone could experience. I truly believe that every stripe He took was a reflection of the sins we'd commit. He took a stripe for adultery, He took a stripe for fornication. He took a stripe for lying. He took a stripe for homosexuality. He took a stripe for cheating. He took a stripe for lasciviousness. He took a stripe for stealing. He took a stripe for covetousness. He took a stripe for procrastination. He took a stripe for all the sins we have and will ever commit, so that we could come boldly to the throne and be reminded of the cross where He died that we might be free. All of this, and yet, He never said a word. Not even the constant beatings and torturing was enough to interrupt His journey to Calvary; eventhough the cross He carried added even more to His painful journey. Each step was even more agonizing than the step before, and though He stumbled several times along the way, and though Simon of Cyrene had to help Him carry the cross because it became too overbearing for Him to do alone, He refused to quit because He knew that the entire world needed Him in order to be full benefactors of the salvation He made possible for us to experience. He knew that the Father was depending on Him to be the Saviour of an entire world. He knew that I was going to mess up; He knew that you were going to mess up, so that's why He kept enduring the pain and the shame and the mocking and the beating and the spitting and the humiliation. He loved us too much to give up now! He knew that the blood was the lifeline for our sickness, for every weapon formed against us, for every lie told to us, for every trap set for us, for every mountain we had to climb over and every valley we had to toil through. He knew that our enemies would have a field day over our demises and failures. He knew that if He kept on walking, if He kept on enduring, and that if He could just make it to Calvary, it would be FINISHED!!!!!!!!!!!!!! The Father's will would be done!!!!!!!!!!!!!! He knew that once they laid Him down and nailed Him to the cross, that He was going to eventually be lifted up! They didn't know what they were doing when they lifted our Savior up. That's why we have been drawn to Him, because they lifted Him up. That's why we can come to Him just as we are because they lifted Him up! That's why I have the right to praise Him; they lifted Him up. That's why though the weapons form, they cannot prosper; they lifted Him up. That's why I know that what's meant for my evil works out for my good every time; they lifted Him up. That's why I can walk by faith and not by sight; they lifted Him up. That's why blessings chase me down; they lifted Him up. That's why I may have been bruised, but I'm never broken; they lifted Him up. That's why I can take a lick and keep on ticking; they lifted Him up. Thank God they lifted Him up, and according to His Word in John 12:32, "And if I be lifted up from the Earth, I will draw all men unto me." Can I also tell you that this was no ordinary cross? This cross was a heavy cross, weighing some 300 lbs. The cross bar itself was said to weigh between 70-90 pounds. This cross is not just a figment of our imagination, nor is it some folktale or myth that's just passed down from one generation to the next. No!! It's much more than that! It's the lifeline to eternal life. It's the cooling water that quenches my thirst; it's the result of the sweet sound I hear whispering in my Spiritually waxed ears when I want to give up because life's problems become overwhelming. It's the effect and assurance that forsakes my will for His will. It's the satisfaction I get when I reflect on the fact that He loved us so much that He willingly gave of Himself when we didn't deserve it then, and still don't deserve it now.

Furthermore, the whip could not be compared to some switch from a tree that we chose whenever we were mischievous. Neither was it a belt from a father's closet, (you know there was a different belt for each circumstance). Jesus didn't get the chance to choose; yet, He remained faithful unto death. As they whipped Him, the flesh fell from His bone. The beating was so horrible that they covered nearly every segment of His body. It was almost as if His entire body was painted with stripes and blood. From His side flowed blood and water. It has been said, yet disputed, that He took 39 lashes. The fact that He took one is enough for me to accept Him as my Lord and Savior. The fact that He would do it all over again is enough for me. The fact that He proved Himself to me that way before I was even born, He knew that I would be born and that despite my foolishness, He still saw something in me that I nor others saw. That's the excitement for me. That's the reality for me. That's the assurance for me. That's the real deal for me. That's what keeps me going. That's what fills my Spiritual tank. That's what gives me hope! That's what makes me hush when I want to tell somebody off! That's what makes me smile when I want to cry! That's what causes me to bless Him at all times…UNAPOLOGETICALLY!!!!

CHAPTER 8

# "UTILIZE YOUR DELETE BUTTON"

*2 Timothy 2:22*

*"So flee youthful passions and pursue righteousness, faith, love, and peace, along with those who call on the Lord from a pure heart."*

Having an enormous amount of followers on your social media sites has its pros and cons. On one hand, it allows you to meet people from around the world, or become acquainted or reacquainted with friends and loved ones. On the other hand, it can become dangerous. Many times we accept people who look to be one way, but after conversing with them, we find out who they really are. This is a good time to exercise your right to delete such individuals.

We can all agree that there are some people who will invite you into their world under false pretenses. They claim to have a certain career, to be or not to be married, to drive a certain automobile or live in a mansion, just to entice you. Unfortunately, many have fallen for this trap and are eventually left standing on the corner of disappointment. Yet, there are some who recognize these individuals at once, and delete them just as quickly as they accept their friend request. Some don't even bother to accept the request at all. That's because they have a solid relationship with God and know the Spirit by the Spirit. Investigative shows are filled with episodes where someone befriends others who said just what they wanted to hear. It's filled with someone searching social media for someone who is vulnerable. They start off smooth, and before you know it, you've fallen for them. Before you know it, you're meeting them in some secret location. They turn you away from your friends and loved ones, and they convince you to stop following your dreams because they promise to support you. Unfortunately, many times it's too late to delete them because you've given them too much information to begin with. In order to receive an upgrade, one has to surround himself with people who have their best interest at heart. Again, this can be tricky because some people come into your life to learn just enough about you to share with others, and by the time you figure this out, it's too late.

  I do recognize that life can cause us to become frustrated and lonely at times, and what the devil will do is send someone just when you're at your lowest to contact you through social media to say just what you want to hear. They'll claim to know the answers to all of your problems. They'll even make you think they're in the exact same boat as you are. Before you know it, you've told them all that they need to hear, and after a few interactions on social media, they've gone on to the next victim, leaving you high and dry. Can I suggest to you that sometimes the only person you need to talk to is Jesus? How about hooking up with him? He has the right solution for your problems. He knows how to protect you; He knows how to comfort you, and He knows just what you need, and guess what? He's not someone who will lead you astray. He's not someone who will love on you one day and drop you like a hot potato the next. No! He's a very present help! Not only that, but your secrets are safe with Him. Is there anyone you need to delete from your life? Is there anyone with whom you need to draw a line in the sand? Is there anyone you need to say, "See ya, wouldn't wanna be you" to? I believe you will feel a lot better when you do. I believe you will sleep better at night when you do. I believe you will recognize that God wants you to accept Him to heal your hurts and get you back on track. If He can't do it, no one else can. Make a list of the people who have just worn you out, who have told you one lie after the other, and who only come to you when they need another favor; yet, when you're in need, they're nowhere to be found. It doesn't even have to be a monetary need; it can be emotional support, and once you've deleted them, don't feel guilty! You can still love them, but for your peace, you may just have to do it from a distance.

## CHAPTER 9

# "FACE THE BOOK"

*Hebrews 4:12*

*"For the word of God is quick, and powerful, and sharper than any twoedged sword, piercing even to the dividing asunder of soul and spirit, and of the joints and marrow, and is a discerner of the thoughts and intents of the heart."*

The Word of God was never intended for us to pick and choose scriptures to satisfy our flesh. The Word of God was intended for us to learn all we can about God, and to obey His every command. At some point in our lives, the Word can be a hard pill to swallow, but when we truly love God, we yearn for Him and His Word. I believe that God's Word is clear, and that it was written by men inspired by God, and when reading it, many secrets can unfold if we're willing to "face the book."

When facing the book, one has to take a complete inventory of himself in order to right his wrongs. We have to be willing to accept what God has laid out for us without compromise, and we have to know that His Word will never steer us wrong. There have been many times in my life where I tried to justify my shortcomings, but I soon learned that I could not justify sin; I had to call it what it was… Sin! I had to accept the fact that either I was going to get in alignment with His Word, or I was surely going to be sorry in the long run.

No doubt, the world has introduced us to various ungodly ways of life, and because the world says it's ok, if we're not careful, we'll think it's okay just because so many others say so. Many times I'm accused of being judgmental. I've also been asked the question, "Have you been saved all of your life?" I chuckle at the questions because sometimes it's the very same people who claim to be saved like me asking them.

Whatever happened to, "Be not conformed to this world, but be ye transformed by the renewing of your mind?" (Romans 12:2). Or, "If any man be in Christ Jesus, He's a new creature; old things are passed away, and behold, all things become new. (2 Corinthians 5:17). Or how about, "Be ye Holy, for I am Holy?" (1 Peter 15:16). Or "Be ye steadfast and immovable, always abounding in the work of the Lord, for as much as you know, your labor is not in vain in the Lord. (1 Corinthians 15:58). In facing the book, we have to accept Him for who He is; not only that, but we must strive to please Him daily. Should we continue to sin that grace may abound? No! The scripture warns in Romans 6:1-2: "What shall we say then? Shall we continue in sin, that grace may abound? No! God forbid. How shall we that are dead to sin, live any longer therein?" If I say that I love God, yet I love sin, then I must re-examine my decision to serve and accept Him as my Lord. We can't have it both ways; we have to "deny our flesh, take up our cross daily and follow Christ." (Luke 9:23). Is it easy? No, and He never promised that it would be. Will we be ridiculed? Yes, but so was Jesus. Will we falter, sure we will at times, but His grace is sufficient.

Throughout the Bible, men had to face the book and accept the fact that they could not do it all alone. That's one of the great attributes of the Word is that it's used as a mirror to show us our true selves. No matter how much spiritual makeup or spiritual facelifts we have, we are reminded in Psalm 119:16 that, "Thy word is true from the beginning: and every one of thy righteous judgments endureth for ever." There are times when the world introduces us to things that satisfy our flesh in an overwhelming fashion; so much so until we take the Word and twist it around to justify our sins; however, the Word is quite consistent, and there comes a time when we have to "face the book", whether we like it or not. Isn't it amazing that the Word of God has the answer to every question we have? The problem, though, is that we don't always want the truth because it will cause us to take a good look at ourselves, and when we do, we sometimes discover that we are not in alignment with the will of God. It's the mature Christian who will take God at His Word and love Him over their flesh. It's the mature Christian who will say, "Not my will Lord, but thine will be done." (Luke 22:42). It's the mature Christian who will face the book and ask the Lord to mold them and make them and shape them and break them. It's the mature Christian who is willing to die daily so that old things may pass away so that ALL things can become new. It's the mature Christian who says, "Won't you face the book today, my sister, my brother? You'll learn how to love more, forgive more, pray more, endure more, and accept the plan that He has for your life even more."

The Bible was not written to condemn you, but to free you. It wasn't written to frustrate you, but to encourage you; it wasn't meant to bring you sadness, but bring you joy; it wasn't meant to intimidate you, but to inspire you; it wasn't meant to make you quit, but to cause you to endure. I know it's difficult to face the book when you think you have it all together; yet, the Word says that even at our best, we're nothing but "filthy rags in the sight of the Lord." (Isaiah 64:6). I know that many times we want to justify our sins so that we can look, sound and seem Holy, but the Bible reminds us that we have ALL sinned and fallen short of God's glory. I also realize that the masks we often wear are unveiled when we delve into God's Word. Not only that, but once we see the real us, we still have to face the fact that we are yet imperfect and will always need His love to sustain us, His power to strengthen us, His hands to hold us, and His grace and mercy to justify us.

Can I tell you that it's okay to face the book? By facing the book we allow His will, not our will, to be done. When we face the book, we can admit that we are nothing without the Lord. When we face the book, we can experience a Spiritual metamorphosis, and while we may be crushed through the process, when it is complete, we can thank God that we don't look like what we've been through. We can declare like Paul when He admitted in Psalm 119:71, that it was "good that I was afflicted." In fact, I think I'd rather face the book now so that I can face my Savior in peace later. I'd rather be broken now, so that I can be made whole. I'd rather admit that I have not arrived now, than to arrive at the judgment sorry that I had not faced the book when I had the chance.

The Book reveals mysteries of what is to come. It also brings hope to a dying world. It serves as the road map and prerequisite to Heaven. It's the healing for our souls. It's the answer to our prayers. It's the very source from whence we first believed. It's the road signs that drive us to our destination. It's the mirror which allows us to not only see ourselves, but to see Jesus as well.

## CHAPTER 10

# "KEEP YOUR BATTERY CHARGED"

*Philippians 4:11-13*

*Not that I am speaking of being in need, for I have learned in whatever situation I am to be content. I know how to be brought low, and I know how to abound. In any and every circumstance, I have learned the secret of facing plenty and hunger, abundance and need. I can do all things through him who strengthens me.*

How often do you have to charge your cell phone battery? I guess that would depend on the type of phone you have. Some phones charge quickly, while others seem to take forever and a day. Don't you just hate it when your battery runs low and you realize you left your charger at home, and everybody you ask for a charger is either using theirs, or their charger isn't compatible with your phone? I can remember trying to force someone else's cord into my phone hoping that by some stroke of magic, it would charge.

Once I realized that no matter how much I pushed and twisted, the cord resisted.

How often do we attempt to force other things or people to fit into our "Spiritual sockets?" We beg, we justify, we pray, and we often say to ourselves, "If I can just get him or her, I know I can change them." I know they'll learn to love me. I'll work hard at it. I'll cook for them. I'll clean for them. I'll run their bath water for them. I'll treat them like a king or queen, and even if I have to force them into my life, I don't care, because it will all be worth it. I know I can make them change, after all, God gives me the desires of my heart; after all, I've never seen the righteous forsaken; after all, I was always told that I could name it and claim it. When we begin to utilize the spiritual cords that God has distributed us to be inserted into the outlet that God intended, we will save ourselves unnecessary stress and disappointment. Remember that God knows the plans He has for you, and yes, these plans revolve around every aspect of your life.

I'm so glad that I don't need a phone charger to get charged up for Jesus. I'm so glad that no matter what type of situation I may find myself in, I can get a Spiritual "jump off". Well, what do you mean about that, Elder? I'm so glad you asked.

Our world is ever changing, and as it changes, we all have to find a way to adapt. The one sure thing we can depend on though is the constant outpouring of love we get to experience from the prince of love Himself, Jesus Christ. Like our cell phones, we are able to determine how much juice we have left before we run completely out. Our cell phones will alert us when we're at 10%, 20%, 50%, or even 100%. Even at that 100%, we have to monitor our usage so that our batteries don't run low again. Likewise, our spiritual batteries have to also be monitored so that when we become weak, we can find strength by going to the source of our strength and the strength of our lives.

You know, God has blessed me with the most amazing family and friends that anyone could ask for. We may have disagreements at times, but whenever one of us needs a "Spiritual Jump," we go into our "Spiritual drawers or cabinets" to pray until we find the right charger to fit our circumstances.

Each morning at 6:00 (Eastern), I, along with my family and friends, meet on a conference call to pray for ourselves, our families, our jobs, our government, and much more. This helps to keep our batteries charged. We recognize that storms are going to come, but we don't wait until the storm comes to pray, we pray before and during the storms. We don't wait to thank Him when He brings us through the storms, but instead, we praise Him smack dead in the middle of the storms. Not only that, but I have several prayer partners who lift me up in prayer throughout the day, because they recognize that with the cares and challenges we are confronted with today, we need all the prayers and support we can receive. No doubt, we need one another. The secret to getting a jump from others is to be sure we know who's charging us. When a battery is being charged, several events are taking place, but the one thing that intrigues me most is that the battery won't give off false signals, making you think you're ready to drive off before time.

A few months ago, I had to have a jump off. Although my car has less than 100,000 miles on it, my battery was beginning to weaken. Once charged, the gentleman told me to not stop, because if I stopped, my battery would die again. Ok! Revelation time! Sometimes we may need a "Spiritual jump." In other words, I may get weak along the way and need another blood-bought believer to use his/her more charged battery to encourage me while I'm going through. Every now and again, I may need to hear the words, "Whatever you do, don't stop, because your battery will die again."

When we take our eyes off of our visions, we give the devil permission to destroy them. When we stop operating in the supernatural, we give him permission to watch us walk after our flesh and not the Spirit. When we begin to say we can't, the devil is right there agreeing with us. Quit selling yourself short. Quit giving up so quickly. Quit using your battery for "foolery", and fix your eyes on the author and finisher of your faith. Spend time with Him; He wants to hear from you; He wants to be a part of your Spiritual growth; He wants to see you "prosper and be in good health even as your soul prospers." (3 John 1:2). He wants you to be the head and not the tail and above and not beneath, but in order to receive these pleasures forevermore, you've got to keep your battery charged. How do I do that, Elder? I'm so glad you asked. You've got to spend time seeking His face. You've got to surround yourself with people who walk by faith and not by sight. You've got to be intentional about studying His Word and spending quality time with Him, so you can hear Him tell you your next move. You've got to, "Acknowledge Him in all of your ways, so He can direct your path." (Proverbs 3:6). You've got to use social media to lift one another up and not tear one another down! You've got to love Him and sing songs unto Him and tell others about His goodness. You can never, ever become ashamed of Him because He warns us in His Word that if we're ashamed of Him before men, that He would be ashamed of us before His Father. (Luke 9: 26-27). For whosoever shall be ashamed of me and of my words, of him shall the Son of man be ashamed, when he shall come in his own glory, and in his Father's, and of the holy angels.(King James Version).

You can't afford to look like your battery is low, and even if it is, you've got to allow the Lord to recharge it. Help me out somebody. Can you just take a few seconds to thank Him for being good? Can you thank Him because in the midst of all the hell you've been through, you kept your battery charged because you realized that it wasn't about you? Can we just agree that God makes no mistakes and that our trials come to make us strong? No wonder James challenges us with these words in (James 1: 2-4) : "My brethren, count it all joy when ye fall into divers temptations. Knowing this, that the trying of your faith worketh patience. But let patience have her perfect work, that ye may be perfect and entire, wanting nothing." So, I challenge you right now to check your Spiritual battery to make sure that it's charged, and if it's not charged, ask the Holy Spirit to help you, so that you can be prepared for what is to come.

## CHAPTER 11

# "WATCH WHAT YOU POST"

*Ephesians 4:29*

*Let no corrupting talk come out of your mouths, but only such as is good for building up, as fits the occasion, that it may give grace to those who hear.*

I'll admit that I love posting messages and pictures on social media, and while I love posting, I realize that it is very important that I watch what I post. I try very hard not to post anything that will compromise my relationship with God; therefore, I can't just post any old thing on social media. Likewise, I am also very careful how I respond to others on social media. There are times that I do comment on posts that are not a true reflection of who I am, but I choose my words very carefully.

In my humble opinion, social media can cause more harm than good. For some, this platform is just a means of airing dirty laundry; yet, for others, it's a time to pray and witness. This is where our true character is revealed. At some point, we have to stop using excuses to justify our actions; for example, just because someone else posts an unfavorable message doesn't mean we have to respond in the same manner. By doing this, we can get our message across and be a witness at the same time.

It's a known fact that employers use social media to determine whether they want applicants to represent them. I guess you can call this a new form of background check. Your social media page can show an employer all they need to know. For them, it won't matter how much experience you have, what school you attended, or whether you graduated Magna Cum Laude, Summa Cum Laude, or "Thank you Lawdie!" Your interview could be most impressive as well, but the true test will come when your social media platform has been unveiled. So the question is, "Is it worth it?" Do you *always* have to respond to negative posts? Do you *always* have to get the last say? Did you have to say what you said in the manner in which you said it? Did you have to speak too hastily, adding even more fuel to the fire?

What if a person is truly at their wits end with nowhere else to turn? What if they need guidance, and instead, you ignore them and scroll down to read your more important messages? You see, ministry takes on many forms. I don't have to be in your physical presence to minister to you; I can use the comment's section of FaceBook; I can text you to let you know that God laid you on my heart; I can pick up my cell phone, call you, pray with you, and assure you that everything is going to be alright. Come on now! The Holy Spirit is not confined to the four walls of the church. He's ever active, present, willing and able to deliver you from the things that have come to destroy you. Please receive this message in the name of Jesus!

I've heard of people going to "Facebook jail" for posting inappropriate messages. Even those who invented social media are mindful that some things are just better left unsaid. Even they obviously have integrity and character when others don't. Well, sometimes God will place us in a "Spiritual Jail" until we can learn to bridle our tongues. Sometimes He'll have us confined so that we can build up our most Holy faith so that the Spirit can teach us to know when to speak and when to be quiet. Sometimes, He has to break us down to build us up in order to restore our broken Spirits, and the only way He can do this is to allow us to experience hardships that will lead us back to Him. It's not necessary to respond to every post, especially when they cause you to compromise your commitment to Christ. Sometimes you have to pray for that person's soul, that God can use their boldness for Him. The Lord just spoke to me and said to inform you that you don't have to share every post either. Share posts that will lift peoples' Spirits. What happens is that when we share posts, that person will share it and it becomes like a domino effect, and the devil is somewhere laughing because he's used one person to post something that should have been left unsaid, to satisfy the flesh of others who have no desire to walk after the Spirit.

Well, can you please post and share this for me? Can you make it your status? Can you ask others to share for me that Matthew 6:33 declares to, "Seek ye first the kingdom of God and His righteousness, and all things shall be added unto you." Can you post and share for me that according to Romans 6:23, "For the wages of sin is death; but the gift of God is eternal life through Jesus Christ our Lord?" Can you post and share that Hebrews 10:38 declares that, "The just shall live by faith?" Can you please post and share for me that Romans 8:28 wants us to be encouraged in knowing that, "All things work together for good to them that love God, to them who are called according to His purpose?" Will you please take a moment to post and share John 3:16 which declares that, "For God so loved the world that He gave His only begotten son; that whosoever believeth in Him should not perish but have everlasting life?" Would somebody please join me in changing the trajectory of social media? Can we make a commitment to stand for Jesus, even if we have to stand alone? Can we stop responding to ungodly posts? When we cease to do so, others will see Christ in us, and they too will begin to "watch what they post!"

CHAPTER 12

# "HE'S NEVER OUTDATED"

*Hebrews 13:8*
*King James Version*
*Jesus Christ is the same yesterday, and today, and forever.*

Times change, people change, seasons change, and fashions change, but there's one thing that will never change...the promises of God. He's never outdated, either; as the scripture above states, "He's the same yesterday, today and forever." (Hebrews 13:8). The problem is that we assume that when things around us change, we can place God in the same category of change. Let's be clear; God's Word will NEVER change!

I often hear people say that we are in a different dispensation! Well, if that's the case, shouldn't we be praying harder? Shouldn't we be casting out demons in the name of Jesus? Shouldn't we be prophesying and having dreams and visions more regularly? I mean, since He's not going to ever change, can we agree to let not our will be done, but His? Can we stop justifying our lifestyles and hold fast to the fact that unless we repent, we shall surely answer to Him on the day of judgment? I mean, can we not just go to church, but be the church. Can we take a stand for what's right instead of agreeing with what's wrong? Can we be frank with our children and tell them that just because the world is doing it doesn't mean that it's right? Can we go back to praying and rebuking every demon that has made himself comfortable in our homes? Can we rebuke that demon that has attached himself to our children? Can we stop trying to pretend that we don't have issues so that God can strip us down and clothe us with righteousness? Can we for once be for real for real? It's not God's desire to get in line with the world, but it should be the world's desire to get in line with Him, and if we're waiting for Him to say yes to sin, then we'll be waiting for a mighty long time.

The Lord isn't calling for us to justify our sins; He's waiting for us to confess them. He's not looking for us to focus so much on our sins that we forget to focus on the one who died so that our sins may be forgiven. Yes! Others may try to convince us to believe that Christianity is outdated, and that Jesus is just a mere man and that the sun didn't refuse to shine, and that the veil didn't rip from top to bottom; they may continue by suggesting that there's no way He could have really conquered death, hell and the grave, and that His last words were not, "It is finished!" I rebuke those lies, because I have too much Word, faith and experience in God to believe otherwise.

When He said that it is finished, I'm convinced that what the devil used to destroy me is finished. Why? Because it was settled on the cross. That, my friend, is not an indication that the plan of salvation is outdated, but instead, it's a profound indication that our Savior lives, and that He has never been, nor will He ever be outdated. Moreover, it's the ultimate urge I hold so dearly that solidifies my deepest desire to be more concerned about how many followers I can encourage to follow Jesus rather than the number of followers I invite to follow me. Why? Because He's not outdated. If He's outdated, what makes me want to love my enemies? If He's outdated, who's this living in me? If He's outdated, who wakes me up in the mornings? If He's outdated, why do I possess the gift of prophecy and this gift of laying hands on the sick and speaking life into dead situations? If He's outdated, why am I running and not becoming weary and walking and not fainting? If He's outdated, who's this making a way out of no way for me? Who's providing for me and keeping me and speaking to me throughout the day, and ordering my steps, and strengthening me where I'm weak and building me up where I'm torn down? Why am I still satisfied with Jesus alone? Jesus Christ will never become outdated; yes, our followers may want to follow us no more because of some vicious rumor they heard and not witnessed, and we may be persecuted for Christ's sake, but in the end, because He lives, we will never be forsaken.

CHAPTER 13

# "HE KEEPS TRACK OF ME

*Psalm 27:5-6*

*King James Version*

*For in the time of trouble he shall hide me in his pavilion: in the secret of his tabernacle shall he hide me; he shall set me up upon a rock. ⁶ And now shall mine head be lifted up above mine enemies round about me: therefore will I offer in his tabernacle sacrifices of joy; I will sing, yea, I will sing praises unto the Lord.*

A few months ago, I left home and set off on a trip. I was dealing with some really pressing issues, and I needed to get away. I noticed how calm my youngest daughter, Destiny, was about my sudden departure. She was as cool as a cool cucumber, and it wasn't until later that I discovered why.

When I returned home, she informed me that she knew exactly where I had gone because of the tracker I had on my phone. She rubbed it in even more when she told me that she started to get her brother to drive her to the place where I had escaped, call me up, and say, "Mom, we're downstairs!" What could I say? I was busted.

Many times we try to escape God, but how many of you know that He knows where you are at all times? Even when we try to escape His presence, since we belong to Him, He takes pleasure in keeping track of us. Although my trip was a physical one, there are times when we also need to escape from the clutter in our minds which keeps us from connecting with Jesus on a deeper level. Sometimes we may need to declutter our physical ears so that we can hear where He's telling us to go and what to do. Because He keeps track of us, we don't ever have to be afraid of the "noisome pestilence" which flies at noonday.

We don't have to be afraid of the arrows that fly over us, because we dwell in a secret place. Don't get me started about the secret place. It's that place where your heart meets God's heart, and you tell Him all of your secrets, though He already knows them. It's that place where you come to Him bare and not ashamed. It's that place where you are so desperate that the only place you want to be is in His presence because you know that, "In His presence is fullness of joy; at thy right hand there are pleasures forever more." (Psalm 16:11). You know that when you can escape to your secret place the way you did when you were a child, you can get in touch with the Savior. You know that your escape is your escape, and it really has nothing to do with anyone else but you and God. It's the time for Him to reaffirm His commitment to you and for you to reaffirm your commitment to Him. It's that place where Mama can't go with you and Daddy can't go with you, and your best friend can't go with you, and your children can't go with you. It's that "steal away" time where you forget about yourself and run to Him. It's that place of desperation where you just lay it all on the line and say, "It is what it is! Lord, I need you! Lord, I can't make it without you. Lord, I want you. Lord, nobody can touch me the way that you touch me because you touch me in that secret, hidden place that only you know about. Touch me Lord in that place that hurts. Massage my heart, oh Lord, and let my heart be pleasing in your sight. Restore unto me the joy of thy salvation, Lord. I'm coming to you with no agenda; I'm coming to you with a broken heart and a contrite Spirit."

You have to come to Him like David, broken to the point where He had no choice but to go to his secret place and call upon the Lord and let him cleanse him with hyssop. I don't know where your secret place is; it may be in your closet where you bow down to Jesus and pour your soul out and just lose yourself in His presence. You may have to strip yourself naked in the Spirit to uncover all the wounds that you've been covering up for days, months and years. You may have to just come clean and tell the Lord that you've sinned against Him and Him alone. Don't think He doesn't already know because He's been keeping track of you. Just like my daughter, Destiny, who declared that she already knew where I had escaped to, and that if she wanted to, she could have driven up to just the place where I went to find refuge. Why? Because she knew how to keep track of me. Did I mention to you that not only was she aware of my final destination, but she also knew exactly where I had stopped along the way?

Shut the front door! Not only does He know the places you have hidden out, but He also knows the places you've visited along the way. Come on here! Some of you have visited places along the way that you had no businesses visiting, but because He was keeping track of you, He didn't allow any evil to befall you. Some of you have picked up "spiritual hitchhikers" along the way, and they robbed you of what rightfully belonged to you. Just because they looked the part and talked the part and walked the part, you allowed them to be a part of your journey, and by the time their true identity was revealed, it was too late because you had already exposed your darkest secrets to them when you should have gone to your secret place where your secrets would remain hidden. You've allowed them to tap into a place that was only meant to be tapped in by Jesus alone, and even though they were packed with a bag or two, they did not have on the entire armour of God, but you gave them a ride anyway, and now, instead of riding, they're driving.

Not to worry though, because even with "spiritual hitchhikers" all round, He still keeps track of you!

## CHAPTER 14

# "ZOOM HIM IN"

*Revelation 3:20*
*King James Version*

*²⁰ Behold, I stand at the door, and knock: if any man hears my voice, and open the door, I will come in to him, and will sup with him, and he with me.*

A few years ago, I was introduced to a program called Zoom! At first, I wanted nothing to do with it, but eventually, I was forced to use it because of the pandemic. After realizing that I had no choice in utilizing it, I began to discover more of its features. One feature I discovered was break-out rooms, and once I mastered it, I began to use it with confidence.

This feature allowed me to assign my students to different rooms according to their specific needs. Before I started writing this chapter of the book, I had to seek the Lord on my way to work and ask what He wanted me to include. He began to speak to me and tell me that there are many times when we need to have Spiritual breakout sessions. I asked what He meant, because I was a bit confused. He began to explain to me that the world has become quite confused. The world says that sin is right when God clearly says that it's wrong.

He continued by saying that it's high time for us to break away from the world and stand on the Word. He said that it's time for us to come together and pray for one another and cast out demons and take Him at His Word. He said it's time for the church to be the church and not just look like the church. He said that too many of us have on garments, but they're not garments of Salvation. He said it's time for us to break away from the world and be ye Holy. He said it's time for us to experience signs and wonders. He said it's time for us to forgive one another and stop gossiping about one another and to begin lifting one another up instead of tearing one another down. He said it's time for us to deny ourselves, and take up our cross and follow Him and to stop being so timid and sensitive and faithless. He's calling for us to speak about life and not death. He's calling for us to go beyond the veil to the Holy of Holies and gas up on our power and be committed to Him. He's calling for us to break away from naysayers who declare that there is no God. He's calling for us to break out of our cocoons and be metaphorically changed and accept the fact that anytime we are being hard pressed, tried, crushed, and broken, that if we can just go through the process, we will soon be what God intended for us to be.

It's time for us to break away from the stain of sin and the lust of our flesh and the cares of this world and have regular sessions with Him. It's time for us to allow Him to look beyond our faults. It's time for us to consider Him again, to trust Him again, to love Him again, to spend time with Him again, and to love Him more than we ever have before.

Just like I was intimidated by using Zoom at first, you may be intimidated by others who seem to have it all figured out. Can I share a secret with you? They may look like it and act like it, but at the end of the day, they too are in need of regular, more intense sessions with God. There's only one perfect person, and His name is Jesus, and He'd love for you to "zoom Him in!

CHAPTER 15

# "GPS" (GUIDING HIS PEOPLE TO SAFETY)

*John 16:13*
*King James Version*

*¹³ Howbeit when he, the Spirit of truth, is come, he will guide you into all truth: for he shall not speak of himself; but whatsoever he shall hear, that shall he speak: and he will shew you things to come.*

The final feature I'd like to share is the GPS. In terms of physical directions, it stands for Global Positioning System; however, I'd like to share with you what GPS means to me. It simply means, "Guiding His People To Safety".

Have you ever been lost before? How did you feel? What did you do? Well, I've been lost on many occasions; not only in a physical sense, but in a Spiritual sense as well. The joy in being lost for me, though, is that whenever I've been lost physically, because God had and still does have a plan for my life, He never allows me to remain lost. Some years ago, prior to GPS, my kids and I traveled to Alabama to visit our family. I had never driven with the kids to Alabama without my husband before, but I thought I was up for the challenge. Going there, we didn't have any problems, but returning was a different experience. As we stopped to gas up, I thought I was headed back on 85 North. Driving along, my son Darius, who was a youngster, but quite observant said, "I could have sworn we came this way already." Initially, I thought, "No we didn't," but I soon began to see familiar sites and realized that he was correct. I got off on the next exit and proceeded to drive in the right direction. Even then, God was guiding me back to safety.

Isn't it something how we can get off track and the devil begins to make us feel that we're on track because he shows us people, places and things that are familiar to us? Sometimes, we recognize what he's doing too late, and before we know it, we're back to doing the same old things we used to do, going the same old places we used to go, and having the same thoughts we had before. I'm so glad that the Lord used our son to realize that we were headed right back to Mobile, Ala.

In the previous chapter, I mentioned "Spiritual hitchhikers". Before you know it, you're allowing them to drop you off at work and keep your car all day and run the gas out, and then when it's time for them to pick you up, they're late and have the audacity to be mad at you because you asked where they've been all day. This is an indication that you were lost and needed the Lord to "Guide you back to safety!

Don't you know how precious you are to Him? Don't you realize that He still has you on His mind? You know, it's one thing to be lost and not know you're lost, but it's a totally different thing when you're lost and know you are, yet you don't want to be found. Luke 19:10 states, "For the Son of Man has come to seek and to save that which was lost." This scripture blows my mind because it clearly suggests that God is not just seeking us just to seek us; He's seeking us to save us. Wow!! He alone knows when we're lost, and He also knows how to find us.

When I was growing up, we had a dog named Penny! I believe she may have been the first dog we ever owned. Once, my sisters had to walk to the library to complete their assignments. Penny followed them, but when it was time for them to leave, Penny was nowhere to be found! Days and weeks passed, but there was no Penny. One day, out of the blue, she showed up. She had found her way back home, and we were ecstatic!! Even our mother, who wasn't really big on dogs, hugged her. We weren't sure of where she had been, neither did we care. We were just happy that she was home. Doesn't that sound just like Jesus? He doesn't care where you've been, He just wants to guide you back to safety. He doesn't care who you've been with; He just wants to guide you back to safety. He knows you messed up; yet, He still wants to guide you to safety. He doesn't even care about how many "spiritual hitchhikers" you've picked up along the way; He wants you to allow Him to pick you up and turn you around. He wants to show you a Spiritual highway; He wants to show you that highway to Heaven where He went to prepare a place for you. You've been riding along lost for sometime now; it's time to be found. You've done it your way for too long now. Do it God's way. Man this thing is deep! Come on, somebody! Come out of sin! There's nothing on that road but destruction and disappointment.

Although I love the fact that my GPS has the ability to get me where I need to go, there are times when danger lies ahead, and I have to be rerouted. I *DREADED* when this would happen to me initially. I mean, I was just getting used to the routed feature, not even considering the fact that at times, I would have to take a different route. I mean, I wanted to go the way I thought it would take me without any issues, but because it didn't, my flesh would rise up.

It wasn't until I received yet another revelation about this unique feature that I was able to fully appreciate its benefits. Simply put, sometimes, there's danger ahead as we journey to our destination, and sometimes we have to reconsider our routes. Well, the GPS knows that, because it has the unique ability to detect this information. Likewise, the Lord, our (GPS), knows as well. Sometimes, the devil will place stepping stones in our path. They could be backstabbers, financial challenges, sicknesses, disappointments, marital issues, children issues, societal issues, and many other unfortunate dilemmas as we travel on this Christian journey. But aren't you glad He knows when, where and how to reroute you? Aren't you happy to know that had you gone the way you had planned, you could have possibly lost your life? Aren't you happy to know that the ever-present God reminds us that He's ours and He knows us by name? Even moreso, He alone wants to be our guide. Come on now! What would we do without Him? How would we live without Him?

Even when He tells us which route to take, we sometimes refuse to listen because many times we think we have it all figured out. But He's so kind that even when we do it our way, He comes to the rescue with outstretched arms to put us back on the right path. That's what happened to Jonah. He didn't want to go where God told him to go to do what God told him to do, but instead, he had a different mindset and ended up in the belly of a fish. But look at God, even though Jonah disobeyed God, God did not hold it against him. He gave him another opportunity to make it right. You may be in an adulterous relationship. Go home to your wife; go home to your husband! You may be a fornicator and you don't want to fornicate anymore, and although the person you're fornicating with doesn't want to stop, the Spirit keeps tugging at you to do the right thing and trust Him. You might be a liar, and nobody can ever believe you because every word that comes out of your mouth is a lie, and so when you finally tell the truth, no one takes you seriously. You may be a thief breaking into folks houses, and you've broken into so many homes that you've lost count. Well, God knows, and He still cares. Make it right with Him! You may even be an atheist and not even believe there is a God. Let Him make Himself known to you. You may be a murderer, and so was Moses, but he still led the children of Israel to the promised land. I don't care which Spiritual interstate you're on; I don't care which city, state or country you're in right now; stop taking the route that will lead to destruction, and allow Him to "Guide You To Safety."

*Dear Reader,*

*Please allow me to thank each of you for your support. I will forever be grateful! I pray that this book has been more of a blessing to you than it has been for me. Just by going in to pay my cell phone bill, the Lord revealed so many things to me in the Spirit. I pray that you were also enlightened; not only that, but I pray that you take each chapter to heart and apply it to every area of your life. I don't care where you are in your walk with Christ, allow Him to lead the way. Perhaps, the devil has made you feel worthless. Well, that's his job, but if you ever dig deep within and allow your true identity to be revealed, you will experience brighter days. Your past will no longer haunt you; you will feel brand new, and you will never, ever be the same again. I invite those of you who may have fallen to the wayside to get back in the race. I don't care how long you've been out, get back in, and take your rightful place. I don't care if you've been offended or misunderstood for trying to do right; give it another try. For those who are depressed and lonely, I invite you to get back up, and live again. Get back up, and hope again. Get back up, and believe again. God is waiting with outstretched arms to receive you even right now. For the remainder of this book, I have elected to share a few poems that I have also written to inspire you along the way. These are my most popular poems, and again, I pray that you find inspiration and hope in each word.*

## "Eligible For An Upgrade"

Luke 4:18

King James Version

"The Spirit of the Lord God is upon me; because the Lord hath anointed me to preach good tidings unto the meek; He hath sent me to bind up the brokenhearted, to proclaim liberty to the captives, and the opening of the prison to them that are bound." (Luke 4:18)."

A few years ago, I jumped out of bed
Got dressed to pay my phone bill
And to my surprise the clerk advised me
Of something that did not seem real

"You're eligible for an upgrade," he began to explain
And I could not believe what I heard
I argued back and forth with him
But he wasn't moved by my words

"I can't be eligible," I said to the man
"For one of my kids just used my upgrade."
But he turned around the screen, and what I had seen
Was exactly what he did state

I finally stopped arguing, but still didn't understand
How I could be eligible so soon
But I paid my bill, and walked out the door
And received a message as clear as the moon

The Spirit spoke to me, and He blew my mind
And said I was eligible in the Spirit as well
I felt joy in my soul that truly overflowed
Because through it all, I was about to prevail

He reminded me of how like I paid my bill
Faithfully and always on time
That He too had been keeping tabs on me
Even when the enemy tried to confuse my mind

He reminded me of how I stood on His Word
And tried to do things His way
And how I strived to live a pure life
Each and every day

So now when the enemy tries to come like a flood
I always reflect on that day
Of when I was told that I was also eligible in the Spirit
And to go ahead and receive my upgrade

A message from God can be found in His text

There's no limit to any of your calls

He's there 24 hours a day

To ensure that you do not fall

No matter what type of phone you may have

Just dial 1-1-1

One for the Father, One for the Spirit

And of course, one for the Son

## "Today, I See The Light"

John 8:12

"When Jesus spoke again to the people, He said, 'I am the light of the world. Whoever follows me will never walk in darkness, but will have the light of life."

Today, I see myself in a different light
The darkness had blinded me all of this time
But now that I see the light
Though it may be distant
I have a smidget of hope
Which is all I needed
To make it through another day
To fall on my knees once again to pray
To believe in me when others don't
To push hard for my every want
Because now, I see the light again
Satan, you should have kept it hidden
And though you did for a while
Now it shines, and again I can smile
Yes, my past was a mess
I did things I should not have done
I went places I should not have gone
I hung with people who weren't meant for me
But I tried to make it work

Because of my bubbly personality

I thought things that I should not have thought

Wasted money buying things I should not have bought

But now, I see the light

And it's beaming radiantly on me

Bringing me hope, bringing me joy, bringing me peace

That light spotlights who I am

And not what I did

Who I am, and not how people perceive me

And though it's been hidden for quite some time

The light is shining, and it's shining on me

And now there's no telling what I can be

## "It's Not Your Final Destination"

Matthew 10:22

"And ye shall be hated of all men for my name's sake: but he that endureth until the end shall be saved."

Don't be so quick to throw in the towel
As if you're in this place to stay;
Don't be so quick to give up on God,
For your destination is farther along the way.
Don't give up on your marriage
For a blessing lies ahead for you;
Don't give up your children,
For a miracle awaits them, too.
Don't give up on your friends,
For a true friend is patient and kind;
And even when your friend has faltered
Their destination too is down the line.
Just don't throw in the towel;
Don't lose your determination,
For the unpleasant place
You find yourself in
Is not your final destination.

Matthew 15:19

"I will give you the keys of the kingdom of heaven; whatever you bind on earth will be bound in heaven, and whatever you loose on earth will be loosed in heaven."

**"Sold"**

Step back satan
And loosen your hold
You can't purchase me
Because I'm already sold

Step back satan
In the name of Christ
Your offers are tempting
But not your price

I didn't have to pay
For the gift I received
All I had to do
Was just trust and believe

Step back satan
Like you have been told
I'm no longer for sale
I've already been sold

## "Meant For Evil, But Worked Out For Good"

Genesis 50:19-20

Joseph said to them, "Do not be afraid, for am I in the place of God? But as for you, you meant evil against me; but God meant it unto good, to bring to pass, as it is this day, to save much people alive."

Disappointing events causing nothing but pain
Could not be understood
The devil meant it for my evil, but God meant it for my good
I'd call my friends and complain to them
About how unfair my situation seemed,
But those who know how much I love the Lord
Knew that somehow I would be redeemed
And there stood God with arms wide open
Waiting to see me through
Just when I thought I could handle no more
He did what He said He would do.
He delivered me through His mighty powers
Right in the devil's face
I now know exactly what the songwriter meant
When he wrote of God's Amazing Grace.
So, if you're in trouble

Don't be afraid,

But trust Him if you would,

And know that what was meant for your evil

Will work out for your good.

## "A Faith Unshaken"

Job 13:15

King James Version

"Though He slay me; yet will I trust in Him." Job 13:15

A faith unshaken is what God wants to see

Even in the midst of a storm;
A faith that surpasses what our eyes have seen
A faith which dismisses all harm
A faith unshaken is when you've done your best
To take God at His word
It's a faith that removes all of your doubts
Despite what you may have heard
It's a faith that stares the doctor in the face
When your results are shown to you
It's a faith that says, "I know a man
Who's able to bring me through."
It's a faith that when the rent is due
And money, you just can't find
It's an unshaken faith in your Spirit which says,
He'll show up right on time
It's a faith which arises when the boss has said,
"I'm sorry, but we have to let you go."
It's an unshaken faith which says to him,
"God is able, I know"

It's a faith that when your children rebel
You still pray for them day and night;
It's a faith that comes in the middle of the night,
And makes everything alright
It's a faith that gives you the strength to face
Any obstacle that comes your way;
It's a faith that deep down inside you know
That God hears you when you pray.